Welcome
TO THE
Seder
A PASSOVER HAGGADAH FOR EVERYONE

RABBI KERRY M. OLITZKY · ARTWORK BY RINAT GILBOA

BEHRMAN HOUSE

www.behrmanhouse.com

For Yonatan Shimon Olitzky and Hannah Faye Olitzky, the newest
in our family to hear the story of the liberation—K.O.

For Ariel—R.G.

EDITORIAL CONSULTANTS:

Rabbi William Cutter, PhD, Steinberg Emeritus Professor of Human Relations,
Hebrew Union College—Jewish Institute of Religion

Keren R. McGinity, PhD, director, Interfaith Families Jewish Engagement,
Shoolman Graduate School of Jewish Education, Hebrew College

Story of Passover retold by Dena Neusner
Editor: Dena Neusner
Art Director: Ann Koffsky
Designer: Zahava Bogner
Editorial Intern: Justin Sagalow
Copyright © 2018 by Kerry Olitzky
Story of Passover copyright © 2018 Behrman House, Inc.
Illustrations copyright © 2018 Behrman House, Inc.
Springfield, NJ

www.behrmanhouse.com

ISBN 978-0-87441-974-0

Printed in the United States of America

LIBRARY OF CONGRESS CATALOGING-IN-PUBLICATION DATA
Names: Olitzky, Kerry M., author. | Gilboa, Rinat, illustrator.
Title: Welcome to the Seder : a Passover Haggadah for everyone / by Rabbi
    Kerry M. Olitzky ; illustrated by Rinat Gilboa.
Other titles: Haggadah.
Description: Springfield, NJ : Behrman House, [2017] | Includes
    bibliographical references.
Identifiers: LCCN 2017033362 | ISBN 9780874419740 (alk. paper)
Subjects: LCSH: Haggadah. | Haggadot--Texts. | Seder--Liturgy--Texts. |
    Judaism--Liturgy--Texts.
Classification: LCC BM674.79 .O45 2017 | DDC 296.4/5371--dc23 LC record available at https://lccn.loc.gov/2017033362

Introduction

Passover is a springtime holiday. And a story about freedom. It traces the Exodus of the Israelites from ancient Egyptian slavery through their journey in the desert to the Land of Israel. Like multihued threads woven into one tapestry, the Israelites were forged into a people. The seder is a structured celebration in which participants reenact that journey as if it were their own. The haggadah is the road map for that journey.

Welcome to the Seder is an inclusive haggadah with which we welcome all those at the table, from the most traditional to first-time seder participants. This haggadah includes many familiar elements of the seder, along with poems, readings, and stories that acknowledge, value, and celebrate the wide range of backgrounds of seder participants today, and inspire us with the universal message of freedom.

There are many ways to conduct a seder. Consider: How will you make this seder your own? Will there be one leader or will everyone take turns reading aloud? Which sidebars will you read? How much time will you allot for questions, debates, singing? You can complete the seder in as little as thirty minutes if you choose. Or, for a more meaningful experience, you can take time to explore the sidebars and questions together, and encourage participants to share their own stories.

MAKE IT UNIQUE

To make the seder different from other meals, you might invite people to come in costumes inspired by the Passover story, or serve food that is informed by a particular cuisine. You can begin the seder in a comfortable place—perhaps the living room or den—and even invite people to sit on pillows on the floor, to set a casual mood. Then move everyone to the dining room for the meal. Your guests might like a dessert bar with Passover-themed treats, such as chocolate frogs or a pyramid made from matzah, chocolate, coconut, and nuts.

SEDER PINEAPPLE

Some people add a pineapple—a
symbol from colonial times signifying
welcome and prosperity—to the seder
table as a message of inclusion to all the
immigrants and refugees in our midst.
We acknowledge their journey and the
obstacles that they have overcome to
reach this country and its promise of
freedom.

Preparing for the Seder

The seder plate is the centerpiece of your table. There are all kinds of seder plates—from homemade, to functional and inexpensive, to handcrafted works of art. Prepare your seder plate in advance, using the items listed on page v.

In addition, you'll need these items on your seder table:

- A plate with three pieces of matzah, under a cover
- A cup, basin, and towel for handwashing
- Extra *charoset*, horseradish, and parsley
- Small bowls of salt water for dipping
- Wine and grape juice
- Elijah's Cup (an extra glass of wine)
- Miriam's Cup (an extra glass of water)
- A haggadah for each participant
- Two candlesticks, candles, and matches
- Pillows or cushions for reclining

RUTH'S CUP

Some people add a Ruth's Cup, filled with wine or grape juice, to signify a welcome to Jews-by-Choice, those who have converted to Judaism, and those of different faiths who share the bonds of family and friendship. This cup is named after the biblical Ruth, a model of kindness and loyalty, who chose the faith of her husband's people.

The Seder Plate

The objects on the seder plate are symbols that help us remember the Passover story.

- **Bitter herbs (*maror*)**—usually horseradish, a reminder of the bitterness of slavery; some seder plates include a second bitter herb, called *chazeret*, which is often romaine lettuce

- *Charoset*—a fruit-and-nut mixture representing the mortar used by slaves in ancient Egypt

- **Leafy greens (*karpas*)**—often parsley or celery, a symbol of springtime renewal; some people use a potato

- **Shank bone (*z'roa*)**—a roasted lamb bone (vegetarians sometimes use a roasted beet), reminiscent of the animal sacrifices that our ancestors made

- **Roasted egg (*beitzah*)**—a roasted, hard-boiled egg, a symbol of life

AN UNUSUAL SEDER PLATE SYMBOL

Some people add an artichoke to the seder plate. "Like the artichoke, which has thistles protecting its heart, the Jewish people have been thorny about this question of interfaith marriage. . . . Let the thistles protecting our hearts soften so that we may notice the petals around us."

—Rabbi Geela Rayzel Raphael and Interfaith Family

AN ORANGE ON THE SEDER PLATE?

Many Passover tables now include an orange on the seder plate. The orange symbolizes the fruitfulness for all when those who have been marginalized are welcomed by the Jewish community. It originated as an affirmation of the roles of women and members of the LGBTQ community. Some families begin the meal by eating the orange and spitting out the seeds to demonstrate their rejection of ideas that have become outmoded.

PASSOVER MIRACLE

for Kara

that we find our spring selves again,
shed the thick protective layers of winter
that shield but separate us
from the world out there.

We sit at the seder table
tired, yes, from all the work of preparation,
but hoping to be refreshed,
hoping in spirit to be refreshed.

Sitting at the seder table
we encounter
our younger selves,
wide-eyed, asking questions.

We become each year once again
the four sons, child-like,
spring-like, ready each year once again
to go out from Egypt

with nothing
but a pack on our back,
ready to walk once again
out into the wilderness

in search of our freedom
and our God.

—Merle Feld

WELCOMING THE STRANGER

"You know what it was like to be a
stranger because you were strangers
in the land of Egypt" (Exodus 23:9). The
Torah mentions "welcoming the stranger"
thirty-six times. (The phrase refers to
outsiders, newcomers, and anyone who
is not familiar to the Jewish community.)
This is more than any other mitzvah or
sacred instruction.

Welcome to the Seder

"This nation . . . will not be fully free until all its citizens are free."—PRESIDENT JOHN F. KENNEDY

At Passover we celebrate the journey of the ancient Israelites from slavery to freedom. It is a universal message for all of us gathered here, and for other seekers of freedom around the world and throughout history.

While we rejoice over the liberation of the ancient Israelites, we remember that many others are still not free. With this seder, we give voice to those around the world and within our community who are excluded, oppressed, or enslaved. We are all part of one human family, all connected, and all responsible for one another.

We welcome each person who sits at our seder table. Each one of us belongs in this ever-expanding community. The future—like the spring that we celebrate this Passover—offers the promise of rebirth, renewal, and hope. Let us remember that rebirth, renewal, and hope must include all of those who do not yet share our freedoms. Let us remember that Passover is not just about who we are, but it is also about what we do. Tonight we celebrate. Tomorrow we act on all that we have learned.

TALK ABOUT IT

What can you do to bring more hope and optimism into the world, beginning with your family or community?

Lighting Candles

"Darkness cannot drive out darkness: only light can do that. Hate cannot drive out hate: only love can do that."—DR. MARTIN LUTHER KING JR.

Light forces darkness to leave. It is also a symbol of the Divine. So we begin the seder by lighting candles, affirming our pledge to bring more light—more knowledge and holiness—into the world.

Light the candles, then recite these words of blessing:

Praised are You, Holy One, Sovereign of the universe, who makes us holy with commandments and instructs us to kindle the (Sabbath and) holiday lights.

Baruch Atah, Adonai Eloheinu, Melech ha'olam, asher kid'shanu b'mitzvotav v'tzivanu l'hadlik neir shel (Shabbat v'shel) Yom Tov.

בָּרוּךְ אַתָּה יְיָ אֱלֹהֵינוּ מֶלֶךְ הָעוֹלָם, אֲשֶׁר קִדְּשָׁנוּ בְּמִצְוֹתָיו וְצִוָּנוּ לְהַדְלִיק נֵר שֶׁל (שַׁבָּת וְשֶׁל) יוֹם טוֹב.

We express our gratitude for this occasion that brings us all together with the words of the *Shehecheyanu* prayer.

Praised are You, Holy One, Sovereign of the universe, who gives us life, sustains us, and has brought us to this moment.

Baruch Atah, Adonai Eloheinu, Melech ha'olam, shehecheyanu, v'kiy'manu, v'higi'anu laz'man hazeh.

בָּרוּךְ אַתָּה יְיָ אֱלֹהֵינוּ מֶלֶךְ הָעוֹלָם, שֶׁהֶחֱיָנוּ וְקִיְּמָנוּ וְהִגִּיעָנוּ לַזְּמַן הַזֶּה.

TALK ABOUT IT
Taking turns around the table, share one thing that you are thankful for today.

Order of the Seder

The word *seder* means "order," and we begin with a list of seder rituals called "the order of the seder." It's like a set of landmarks for the evening that helps us find our place in the haggadah and follow the progress of the seder.

Making Holy: *Kadeish*

Washing: *Ur'chatz*

The Renewal of Springtime: *Karpas*

Separation: *Yachatz*

Telling the Passover Story: *Maggid*

Ritual Cleansing: *Rochtzah*

Eating Matzah: *Motzi Matzah*

The Bitterness of Slavery: *Maror*

Sandwiching the Bitter: *Koreich*

The Meal Is Served: *Shulchan Oreich*

The Afikoman: *Tzafun*

Expressing Gratitude: *Bareich*

Giving Praise: *Hallel*

Seeking Acceptance: *Nirtzah*

Making Holy: *Kadeish*

"The holidays are only holy if we make them so."
—MARIANNE WILLIAMSON

Time can become holy. We elevate distinctive times, such as holidays, by separating them from other times, such as the routine of daily living. We mark the seder as holy time by beginning with a blessing. Our blessings and rituals remind us to focus on this time we have together, to keep it separate from what has come before and what will come after. By joining together around this table in celebration of hope and freedom, we make this time—and this place—sacred.

We will drink four cups of wine or grape juice tonight. The seder is a celebration of freedom, and so with each cup we remember one of four promises of freedom made by God to the ancient Israelites, as recorded in the Torah.

Fill your glass, then raise it while reciting the first promise:

"I will free you from slavery in Egypt." (Exodus 6:6)

WHAT IS OUR SACRED ROLE?

"Because we come from all other peoples, we are bridge-builders and connectors; we are ambassadors and weavers between worlds. Because we live our lives in many different ways, between genders and sexes and varied ways of loving, we stand at the doorway of Possibility, and it is from this that we derive our sacred role as holy people dedicated to truth and integrity, even in the face of death."

—Adapted from *The Stonewall Seder*

Say the blessings:

Praised are You, Holy One, Sovereign of the universe, who creates the fruit of the vine.

Baruch Atah, Adonai Eloheinu, Melech ha'olam, borei p'ri hagafen.

בָּרוּךְ אַתָּה יְיָ אֱלֹהֵינוּ מֶלֶךְ הָעוֹלָם, בּוֹרֵא פְּרִי הַגָּפֶן.

Praised are You, Holy One, Sovereign of the universe, who makes us holy with commandments. Out of love, You have given us (the Sabbath,) times for rejoicing, happy holidays to celebrate, and this Passover holiday, a celebration of our freedom from slavery in Egypt. Praised are You, Holy One, who makes holy (the Sabbath,) our community, and festivals.

Make yourself comfortable as you drink the first of four cups of wine or grape juice.

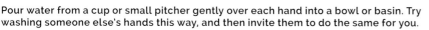

Washing: *Ur'chatz*

"Water is the beginning of all things."—THALES OF MILETUS (CA. 624–546 BCE)

Water cleanses. Water purifies. Thus, we begin the seder by washing our hands, symbolically removing the impurities of the material world. While there are no words of blessing for this ritual, when we pour water for one another, it transforms our actions into blessing. Through this ritual, we bless one another.

Pour water from a cup or small pitcher gently over each hand into a bowl or basin. Try washing someone else's hands this way, and then invite them to do the same for you.

No splashing please!

NATIVE AMERICAN CLEANSING RITUALS

Among many native American tribes, a variety of ceremonies take place in a sweat lodge, including ritual cleansing. Some tribes, such as the Cherokee, immerse themselves in bodies of water with moving currents, such as rivers or streams, for ceremonies such as namings.

WATER IN CHRISTIANITY

Water initiation rituals are found in many religions and cultures, including the Christian rite of baptism, in which a person is immersed in water to welcome him or her into the faith as a believing Christian.

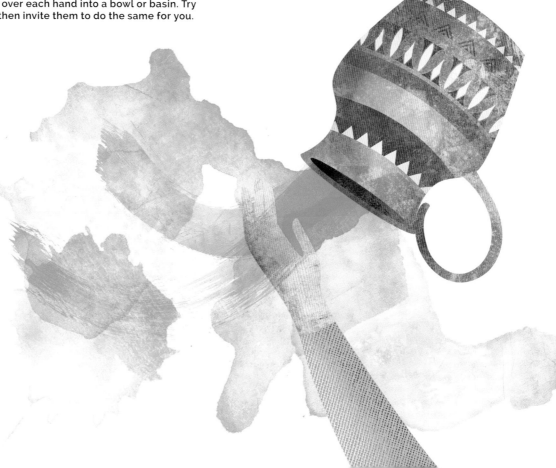

Renewal of Springtime: *Karpas*

NEW DAY

Nowruz, which means "new day," is the Persian New Year celebration, marking the spring equinox in Iran and other countries that have been influenced historically by the Persian religion of Zoroastrianism. Those who celebrate use the occasion to clean their homes, purchase new clothing, visit family and friends, and enjoy a meal with a centerpiece—called *Haft Seen*—consisting of symbolic food items.

"The spring wakes us, nurtures us and revitalizes us."—GARY ZUKAV

Wherever we live, the seasons change. For some, cold winter snows give way to the greening of spring. For others, winter rains are replaced by gentle breezes and long pleasant evenings. The forces of nature are quite powerful, even when they seem mild. Judaism names the author of these laws of nature as God.

Adonai. Eloheinu. Higher Power. Almighty. Savior. Ruler. Lord. Creator. Rock. Shelter. *Sh'chinah*. There are many names for God. Each reflects one of the many ways we experience the Divine in our lives. As you sit around the seder table and taste the sweetness of spring and of freedom, what name would you offer for that power beyond the self? You may want to use that name as you recite the blessing over *karpas*, the leafy greens.

TALK ABOUT IT

The *karpas* is a sign of spring. What other signs of spring, of renewal, do you see around you?

Take a sprig of parsley or other greens from your seder plate.
Dip the greens in salt water. Recite these words of blessing:

Praised are You, Holy One, Sovereign of the universe,
who creates the fruit of the earth.

Baruch Atah, Adonai Eloheinu, Melech ha'olam,
borei p'ri ha'adamah.

בָּרוּךְ אַתָּה יְיָ אֱלֹהֵינוּ מֶלֶךְ הָעוֹלָם, בּוֹרֵא פְּרִי הָאֲדָמָה.

Now you may eat the greens.

No making faces!

Separation: Yachatz

WHAT DOES THE MATZAH REPRESENT?

Some say the three pieces of matzah represent the variety of people in the Jewish community. (Although to really represent the diversity, we would need many more pieces!) The bringing together of the three pieces suggests to us that we are all on this journey to freedom together.

"We only reach wholeness and joy by integrating the stories of brokenness into our stories of liberation."—RABBI MYCHAL COPELAND

Uncover the plate of matzah. Break the middle matzah into two pieces. Put the smaller piece back, and wrap the larger piece, the *afikoman*. Then ask someone to hide the *afikoman*. After dinner, the children will search for it and return it for a reward so that we can complete the seder. In some families, the children hide the *afikoman* and the adults find it.

We break the middle matzah as a reminder that our world is not whole as long as there is suffering and injustice. Just as the lives of the ancient Israelites were transformed by their Exodus from Egypt, we too can find healing, for ourselves and for others, by working for freedom and an end to suffering and injustice.

Telling the Story: *Maggid*

"Days are scrolls. Write on them what you want to be remembered."—BACHYA IBN PAKUDA

Called *maggid* in Hebrew, the story section forms the core of the Haggadah. This is the story of the Exodus from Egypt, and how the ancient Israelites got there in the first place. Matzah is an important part of that story.

Raise the plate of matzah and say:

This is the bread of poverty that our ancestors ate in the land of Egypt. Let all who are hungry come and eat. Let all who are in need come and celebrate with us. Now we are here; next year may we be in the Land of Israel. This year we are still slaves; next year may we be truly free.

Ha lachma anya di achalu avhatana b'ar'a d'Mitzrayim.

הָא לַחְמָא עַנְיָא דִּי אֲכָלוּ אַבְהָתָנָא בְּאַרְעָא דְמִצְרָיִם.

TALK ABOUT IT

What can you do tomorrow, after our seder is over, to reach out to those who do not have what they need?

WISDOM, UNDERSTANDING, AND KNOWLEDGE

Mystics name the bottom piece of matzah "knowledge," the middle piece "understanding," and the top piece "wisdom." We each strive to make our way up through these spiritual levels until we are able to reach the top level and find the place where we belong—closer to all that is sacred.

The Four Questions

The Four Questions prompt us to retell the Passover story that follows. Whether we know the story well from years past, or it's entirely unfamiliar to us, we can learn something new each time we hear it.

In many families, the youngest participant is asked to recite the traditional Four Questions. In others, they are recited in unison. You may want to invite seder participants to ask their own questions about the story and the journey of the ancient Israelites from Egypt.

Parents: You're probably used to your children asking lots of questions!

How different is this night from all other nights!

1   On all other nights, we eat either bread or matzah.
    Why do we eat only matzah, unleavened bread, tonight?

2   On all other nights, we eat all kinds of vegetables and herbs.
    Why do we eat only bitter herbs tonight?

3   On all other nights, we usually don't dip our herbs at all.
    Why do we dip our herbs twice tonight?

4   On all other nights, we eat either sitting up straight or reclining.
    Why do we recline at the table tonight?

Ma nishtanah halailah hazeh mikol haleilot!

1 *Sheb'chol haleilot anu och'lin chameitz umatzah. Halailah hazeh kulo matzah.*

2 *Sheb'chol haleilot anu och'lin sh'ar y'rakot. Halailah hazeh maror.*

3 *Sheb'chol haleilot ein anu matbilin afilu pa'am echat. Halailah hazeh sh'tei f'amim.*

4 *Sheb'chol haleilot anu och'lin bein yoshvin uvein m'subin. Halailah hazeh kulanu m'subin.*

TALK ABOUT IT
Taking turns around the table, ask questions that you have always wondered about Passover. Figure out the answers together, if you can.

מַה נִּשְׁתַּנָּה הַלַּיְלָה הַזֶּה מִכָּל הַלֵּילוֹת!

1 שֶׁבְּכָל הַלֵּילוֹת אָנוּ אוֹכְלִין חָמֵץ וּמַצָּה. הַלַּיְלָה הַזֶּה כֻּלּוֹ מַצָּה.

2 שֶׁבְּכָל הַלֵּילוֹת אָנוּ אוֹכְלִין שְׁאָר יְרָקוֹת. הַלַּיְלָה הַזֶּה מָרוֹר.

3 שֶׁבְּכָל הַלֵּילוֹת אֵין אָנוּ מַטְבִּילִין אֲפִילוּ פַּעַם אֶחָת. הַלַּיְלָה הַזֶּה שְׁתֵּי פְעָמִים.

4 שֶׁבְּכָל הַלֵּילוֹת אָנוּ אוֹכְלִין בֵּין יוֹשְׁבִין וּבֵין מְסֻבִּין. הַלַּיְלָה הַזֶּה כֻּלָּנוּ מְסֻבִּין.

TALK ABOUT IT
Imagine a fifth child. What kind of child might this be? How would you teach this child?

The Four Children

As we answer the Four Questions—and tell the Passover story—we are guided by the many ways each of us learns. Our tradition teaches that there are four different kinds of children, and we should teach each one according to his or her needs. Today we recognize that every child is unique, with an unlimited variety of characteristics. There is a bit of these four children in each and every one of us, no matter our age. Wherever our personal journeys may take us, we are always welcome home and at this table.

Invite individual participants to read aloud the paragraphs below, feeling free to add their own words and ideas.

The wise child asks, "What are the stories, laws, and judgments that God has instructed?"

I am the one you call wise. I have learned to honor the traditions of my parents and their ways, and to value the path that they have shown me. I thirst for more knowledge about my past and my people. Teach me everything.

The rebellious child asks, "What does this service mean to you?"

I am the one you call "rebellious" and sometimes "wicked." I have chosen my own course in life, distant from what others had hoped for me. Accept me as I am, even if you don't always like the decisions I have made.

The innocent child asks, "What is this?"

I have been protected from the world and have stayed close to what is most familiar to me. I am happy with what I have been given and thankful for it. But as I grow older, I yearn for connections to my family and community. Teach me, and reassure me.

The fourth child is unable to ask.

I am unable to ask about why we are gathered together and what this gathering has to teach me, how it can prepare me for life ahead. Show me by example. Help me to grow.

TALK ABOUT IT
Who in your community is marginalized? What can you do to include them, during and after the holiday?

We Were Slaves

As we tell the Passover story, we remind ourselves with the words of *Avadim Hayinu* that we were once slaves:

We were slaves to Pharaoh in Egypt, but God brought us out with a strong hand and an outstretched arm. Had God not brought us out of Egypt, then we and our children and our children's children would still be slaves.

Avadim hayinu, hayinu. Atah b'nei chorin, b'nei chorin.

עֲבָדִים הָיִינוּ, הָיִינוּ, עַתָּה בְּנֵי־חוֹרִין, בְּנֵי־חוֹרִין.

Promises

The ancient Israelites were able to believe in a future when they would be free, even though the surrounding world seemed dark and dismal. That is their gift to us and the lesson of the seder: optimism even in difficult circumstances. Such belief can help us maintain our faith in ourselves and in the community of family, friends, and neighbors who gather around us this evening. Such belief can motivate us to action. Such belief can empower us to do great things, such as freeing slaves and building a nation.

Raise your glass of wine or grape juice. Read these words:

The promise of freedom has been a source of strength to our ancestors and to us.

V'hi she'amdah la'avoteinu v'lanu.

וְהִיא שֶׁעָמְדָה לַאֲבוֹתֵינוּ וְלָנוּ.

Return your cup to its place.

TALK ABOUT IT

How can a promise be a source of strength to a person and a community? What promises sustain you now?

The Story of the Exodus

The story of how the Israelites became a free people is the heart of the haggadah. The Torah sums up the story with these words:

> "My ancestor was a nomadic Aramean [probably from an area that is now modern Syria]. With only a few people, he went down to Egypt and lived there. My ancestors became a great nation there—mighty and numerous. But the [ancient] Egyptians were cruel to us, and they forced us to work as slaves. We cried out to Adonai, the God of our ancestors. God heard our cry and took note of how painful our lives had become. With a mighty hand, with an outstretched arm, with awesome power, and with wondrous examples of heavenly might, God took us out of Egypt." (Deuteronomy 26:5–8).

We begin our story in the Land of Israel, formerly called Canaan. There was famine in the land, and the people suffered greatly. Our ancestor Jacob learned that there was plenty of food in Egypt, a country to the south of Canaan. So he brought his entire family to live in Egypt, where his son Joseph was the prime minister, second in power only to Pharaoh.

TALK ABOUT IT

As former slaves, we remember what it was like to be unwelcome as foreigners, thought of as strangers in ancient Egypt. Thus, we are instructed to "welcome the strangers" in our community. Who are these strangers today? What can you do to welcome them?

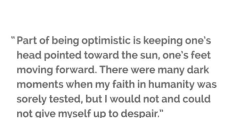

Years later, a new Pharaoh arose over Egypt, who knew nothing of Joseph. This Pharaoh could not see the contributions the Israelites had made to Egypt since the time of Joseph. He saw only a foreign people whose numbers were growing, and he was afraid. He forced the Israelites into slavery, to build his cities and to break their spirit.

The Egyptians set harsh taskmasters over the Israelites. The slaves made mortar and bricks, and worked the fields until they collapsed from exhaustion. But the Israelites kept their faith and their ways, and, despite their suffering, they continued to grow in number. Pharaoh was even more afraid and was determined to destroy them. He ordered the Hebrew midwives Shiphrah and Puah to kill all the Israelite baby boys when they were born. But the midwives had courage and refused to do his bidding. Then Pharaoh ordered that every newborn baby boy be thrown into the Nile River.

The Israelites were determined to protect their children in any way possible. One Israelite mother, Yocheved, placed her son in a basket in the Nile River. She sent her daughter, Miriam, to hide in the bushes and watch over him. Pharaoh's daughter came to bathe in the river and found the baby. Defying her own father's cruel decree, she adopted the child. She called him Moses, which means "drawn from the water." Miriam offered to bring an Israelite woman to nurse the baby, and Pharaoh's daughter agreed. And so Yocheved herself nursed baby Moses.

> "Part of being optimistic is keeping one's head pointed toward the sun, one's feet moving forward. There were many dark moments when my faith in humanity was sorely tested, but I would not and could not give myself up to despair."
>
> —Nelson Mandela

Moses grew up as a prince in the royal palace. But he had a kind heart and could not ignore the suffering of his people. One day he saw a master beating an Israelite slave. He stepped in to defend the slave, and in his anger he struck the Egyptian and killed him. Afraid for his life, Moses fled Egypt. He settled in the land of Midian, where he worked as a shepherd, and married Zipporah, the daughter of a local priest. One day, while his sheep were grazing on the side of a hill, Moses saw an amazing thing: a bush that seemed to be on fire, but its branches did not burn up.

God called Moses from the midst of the flames, and Moses said, "Here I am." God told Moses, "I have seen the suffering of My people. Go to Pharaoh, and then bring the Israelites out of Egypt." But Moses was afraid, protesting, "I am not a man of words." So God directed Moses's brother, Aaron, to go with him.

Moses and Aaron went to Pharaoh and demanded that he let the Israelites go free. But Pharaoh refused and, instead, made the slaves work even harder. So God brought terrible plagues upon Egypt—blood, frogs, lice, flies, cattle disease, boils, hail, locusts, and darkness. Though the people of Egypt suffered with each plague, Pharaoh was stubborn and refused to free the Israelites. Then came the tenth plague, the worst of them all: every firstborn male Egyptian died. A great cry arose from Egypt that night. Finally, Pharaoh allowed the Israelites to leave.

WILD BEASTS OR FLIES
Scholars disagree on the nature of the fourth plague. Is it wild beasts or flies? The meaning of the Hebrew word *arov* has been debated for nearly two thousand years.

The Ten Plagues

Read the list of plagues below one at a time. Each time you read the name of a plague, dip your finger or a spoon into your glass, removing a drop of wine or juice and placing it on your plate.

Blood	*Dam*	דָּם
Frogs	*Tz'fardei'a*	צְפַרְדֵּעַ
Lice	*Kinim*	כִּנִּים
Flies	*Arov*	עָרוֹב
Cattle Disease	*Dever*	דֶּבֶר
Boils	*Sh'chin*	שְׁחִין
Hail	*Barad*	בָּרָד
Locusts	*Arbeh*	אַרְבֶּה
Darkness	*Choshech*	חֹשֶׁךְ
Death of the Firstborn	*Makat B'chorot*	מַכַּת בְּכוֹרוֹת

WHY DO WE DIP?
We remove a drop of wine from our glass at the mention of each plague to demonstrate that our joy is diminished as a result of the pain and suffering of others.

TALK ABOUT IT
Together make a list of things you would bring with you if you had to leave home in the middle of the night and could take only what you could carry.

The ancient Israelites left Egypt in a hurry. They gathered their flocks, they took their bread dough before it could rise, and they raced out of Egypt, joined by some Egyptians and other slaves. But soon Pharaoh regretted his decision. He changed his mind and sent his powerful army after them. The Israelites stopped at the shore of the Red Sea, trapped between the water and the advancing Egyptian army.

God told Moses to raise his staff, and the waters parted. A path opened through the sea, the waters raging on both sides. Jewish tradition tells how the Israelites were afraid to cross, waiting at the water's edge until one man, Nachshon ben Amminadab from the tribe of Judah, bravely entered the water first. The people followed and crossed to safety. The Egyptian army pursued them, but the waters closed in, and the soldiers drowned.

There is a time to think, a time to talk, and a time just to dance. Safe at last, Moses and his sister Miriam led the Israelites in song and dance. They were overwhelmed by joy; they were finally free.

GO DOWN, MOSES

The Exodus story has universal appeal as a story of freedom. Harriet Tubman is known in African American literature as "Moses" for her role in freeing black slaves. When she undertook rescue missions in the South, Tubman sang songs, such as "Go Down, Moses," about the Exodus. She would vary the tempo to indicate whether it was safe or dangerous for slaves to move along the Underground Railroad.

RECLAIMING THE MIXED MULTITUDE

When the Israelites left Egypt, the Torah tells us they were joined by groups of other people, including Egyptians and other slaves, which the Torah calls *erev rav*, or "a mixed multitude." Although some are uncomfortable with this term, we know that when people from diverse backgrounds and traditions join together as a community, we can be optimistic about what the future holds for all of us.

Miriam's Cup

The prophet Miriam watched over her baby brother, Moses, in the Nile, and she inspired the Israelites with song and dance after crossing the Red Sea. According to tradition, a miraculous well accompanied the Israelites in the desert, providing them with fresh water and renewing their spirit until the day Miriam died.

This Miriam's Cup, filled with water, reminds us of her strength and bravery, without which the ancient Israelites may not have survived.

Pass Miriam's Cup around the table and pour a little water into your own water glass. Say the blessing below and then drink.

You abound in blessings, Mother and Father God,

creator of the universe, Who sustains us with living water.

May we, like the children of Israel leaving Egypt,

be guarded and nurtured and kept alive in the wilderness,

and may You give us wisdom to understand

that the journey itself holds the promise of redemption.

AMEN.

—Rabbi Susan Schnur, from *A Miriam Seder, Lilith magazine*

The Rabbis at B'nei B'rak

A story is told about five rabbis at a seder in the town of B'nai B'rak, in ancient Israel. They were so engrossed in the story of the Exodus from Egypt that they stayed up all night discussing it, until their students arrived and said, "Rabbis, it's morning! It's time to say the morning Sh'ma."

What traditional haggadahs don't tell us, however, is that B'nei B'rak was the site of a rebellion against Roman occupation, and the rabbis most likely used their seder not only to discuss the Israelites' freedom from slavery in Egypt, but also to secretly plan their resistance against the Romans. No wonder it took all night!

WHY DO WE RETELL THIS STORY AT THE SEDER?

"This tale may be read as an encouragement to become so joyfully immersed in the seder that we don't notice the passing of time . . . and it may also be read as a story of how one liberation begets another. Celebrating our freedom from servitude can be a radical act. It was Rabbi Akiva, after all, who famously answered the query, 'Which is better, study or action?' with the response, 'Study—if it leads to action.'"

—Rabbi Daniel Gropper

FREEDOM

In remembrance of the 2011 protests in Tunisia, Egypt, Gabon, Bahrain, Libya, and elsewhere.

Liberation comes when people gather

by the tens and by the thousands

demanding that the despot who's held the reins

step down . . .

and members of one faith link hands

to protect members of another faith at prayer . . . .

as real people rise up to say

we have the right to congregate and to speak

we will not be silenced, we are not afraid.

—Rabbi Rachel Barenblat

It Would Have Been Enough: *Dayeinu*

SCALLION WHIPS

It is a custom for Jews from countries such as Afghanistan, Iran, and Iraq to whip each other gently with scallions—to simulate the beating of slaves—during the recitation of "Dayeinu."

Try it. But don't forget to set some rules ahead of time!

It is often hard to know when we have enough—whether in the desert journey of the ancient Israelites or in our current life's journey. The word *dayeinu* means "it would have been enough." The seder song "Dayeinu" reflects our gratitude for all that God did for the Israelites during the Exodus and throughout their desert journey. It also is a prayer for the future—that God (however we define God) continue to remain as a presence in our lives and in history. And it reminds us to express an appreciation for all the blessings we have been given.

We sing the following verses from "Dayeinu" together:

Ilu hotzi-, hotzi'anu, hotzi'anu miMitzrayim, hotzi'anu miMitzrayim, dayeinu.

(Refrain:)
Da-da-yeinu, da-da-yeinu, da-da-yeinu, dayeinu dayeinu.

Ilu natan, natan lanu, natan lanu et haShabbat, natan lanu et haShabbat, dayeinu.

(Refrain)

Ilu natan, natan lanu, natan lanu et haTorah, natan lanu et haTorah, dayeinu.

(Refrain)

Discuss each of the following verses from "Dayeinu." Together, answer the question: Would it really have been enough?

Had God brought us out of Egypt and not divided the sea for us, *dayeinu*, it would have been enough!

Had God divided the sea for us and not led us through on dry land, *dayeinu*!

Had God led us through on dry land and not nurtured us in the desert for forty years, *dayeinu*!

Had God nurtured us in the desert for forty years and not fed us manna, *dayeinu*!

Had God fed us manna and not given us Shabbat, *dayeinu*!

Had God given us Shabbat and not brought us to Mount Sinai, *dayeinu*!

Had God brought us to Mount Sinai and not given us the Torah, *dayeinu*!

Had God given us the Torah and not brought us to the land of Israel, *dayeinu*!

Had God brought us to the land of Israel and not built the Temple for us, *dayeinu*!

For each of these things and for all of them together, we say *dayeinu*.

DAYEINU

"'It would have been enough' does not give us an excuse to be complacent. It does not give us an excuse to stop learning, to stop improving. It does not mean that we should be satisfied with the current state of affairs. Instead, *dayeinu* means that we should take a moment to celebrate and appreciate each step of our personal and collective journey as if it were enough, but then continue on. *Dayeinu* is not about being satisfied with what we have, it's about feeling the fullness of the incomplete and knowing we must push on."

—Sara Greenberg

The Symbols on the Table

According to Rabbi Gamliel, in the Jewish text called the Talmud, no seder is complete until *pesach*, *matzah*, and *maror* are explained.

Point to the shank bone (or beet).

Pesach refers to the shank bone or the beet. This reminds us of the paschal sacrifice—the offering that the ancient Israelites made, according to tradition, before their Exodus from Egypt. They marked their doorposts with the blood of a lamb to signal the angel of death to pass over their homes during the final plague.

Point to the matzah.

***Matzah*,** or unleavened bread, symbolizes the bread of poverty the Israelites ate. They fled from Egypt in such a hurry that they did not have time to let their bread dough rise.

Point to the horseradish.

***Maror*,** or the bitter herb, reminds us of how the Egyptians made the lives of the Israelites bitter with backbreaking work.

TAKE A LOOK
Pass a mirror around the table so that people can see and imagine themselves as personally delivered from Egypt.

In Every Generation

In every generation, each of us should look upon ourselves as if we were personally freed from ancient Egypt.

B'chol dor vador chayav adam lirot et atzmo k'ilu hu yatza miMitzrayim.

בְּכָל דּוֹר וָדוֹר חַיָּב אָדָם לִרְאוֹת אֶת עַצְמוֹ כְּאִלּוּ הוּא יָצָא מִמִּצְרָיִם.

"If your plan is for one year, plant rice.
If your plan is for ten years, plant trees.
If your plan is for one hundred years, educate children."

—Confucius (551–479 BCE)

This is the signature statement of the seder. It is the invisible thread that runs through the entire seder, weaving all of its individual sections together. At the same time, it is a difficult idea for those of us who live freely to understand. How can we consider ourselves slaves when we have never known any form of enslavement?

People can be enslaved in more ways than one—by poverty and inequality; by intolerance and bigotry; by ignorance and fear and hate. When we have the courage to do what is right for ourselves and for others, we are free.

"In every generation" is also a thread connecting one generation to the next, transmitting Jewish identity in whatever form it takes and no matter the shape of the family. Those from other backgrounds enrich our community with the experience of other practices, traditions, and ways of thinking.

Psalms

FOCUS ON FEELING

The book of Psalms, which is sometimes considered Judaism's earliest book of prayers, provides us with words that can help us focus on feelings of gratitude or wonder with *kavanah* (Hebrew for experiencing prayer with intention and feeling). Find a quiet space in your mind. Then pick one line from the psalms on this page to use as your own sacred mantra. Softly repeat the line over and over again, in English or Hebrew, until you can claim the verse as your own.

Praise God from the rising of the sun to its setting.

Mimizrach shemesh ad m'vo'o m'hulal sheim Adonai.

You raise the poor from the dust and lift the needy from the ashes.

M'kimi mei'afar dal, mei'ashpot yarim evyon.

I suffered distress and sorrow. Then I called on Adonai.
Deliver my soul!

Tzarah v'yagon emtza. Uv'sheim Adonai ekra.
Anah Adonai maltah nafshi!

(from Psalms 113–116)

The Second Cup

We raise the second cup of wine or juice, which reminds us of God's second promise to free the Israelites from slavery.

Fill your glass, then raise it while reciting the second promise:

"I will deliver you from slavery." (Exodus 6:6)

Remember to make yourself comfortable. Say the blessing below:

Praised are You, Holy One, Sovereign of the universe, who creates the fruit of the vine.

Baruch Atah, Adonai Eloheinu, Melech ha'olam, borei p'ri hagafen.

בָּרוּךְ אַתָּה יְיָ אֱלֹהֵינוּ מֶלֶךְ הָעוֹלָם, בּוֹרֵא פְּרִי הַגָּפֶן.

Now you can drink, and enjoy, the wine or juice.

"Jewish teaching is more about getting beyond yourself than satisfying your personal desires. It's about connecting, joining, and feeling that much deeper sense of fulfillment and completeness that isn't possible for the solitary individual."

—Dr. Alan Morinis

TALK ABOUT IT

What makes you happy? Share with each other something that recently filled you with joy.

Ritual Cleansing: *Rochtzah*

"We raise our hands in holiness, remembering once again that our liberation is bound up in everyone else's. Each step we take together with others towards liberation is a blessing."

—RABBI MENACHEM CREDITOR

RITUAL WASHING IN ISLAM

Water is important in Islam for cleansing and for removing ritual impurities before performing many religious acts, such as before prayer and before touching the Qu'ran.

We didn't say a blessing when we washed our hands at the beginning of our seder. However, we now say a blessing before washing our hands to acknowledge that the food we are about to eat and the rituals we are about to perform will be raised to a sacred level. In this way, we can become like a nation of priests, those who were responsible for the well-being of our community in ancient times. And our seder table thus becomes like an altar.

Repeat the process of washing your hands as you did at the beginning of the seder. Then raise your hands slightly, as if toward Heaven (in the blessing, the phrase *n'tilat yadayim* literally means to raise up one's hands), and recite the words below:

Praised are You, Holy One, Sovereign of the universe, who makes us holy with commandments and instructs us to ritually wash our hands.

Baruch Atah, Adonai Eloheinu, Melech ha'olam, asher kid'shanu b'mitzvotav v'tzivanu al n'tilat yadayim.

בָּרוּךְ אַתָּה יְיָ אֱלֹהֵינוּ מֶלֶךְ הָעוֹלָם, אֲשֶׁר קִדְּשָׁנוּ בְּמִצְוֹתָיו וְצִוָּנוּ עַל נְטִילַת יָדָיִם.

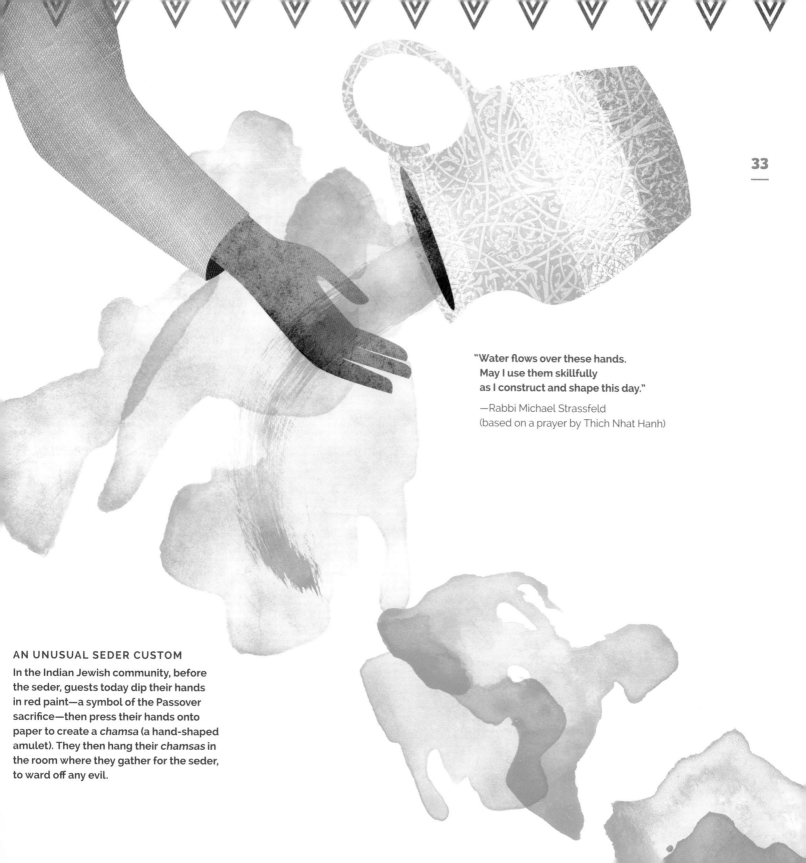

"Water flows over these hands.
May I use them skillfully
as I construct and shape this day."

—Rabbi Michael Strassfeld
(based on a prayer by Thich Nhat Hanh)

AN UNUSUAL SEDER CUSTOM

In the Indian Jewish community, before the seder, guests today dip their hands in red paint—a symbol of the Passover sacrifice—then press their hands onto paper to create a *chamsa* (a hand-shaped amulet). They then hang their *chamsas* in the room where they gather for the seder, to ward off any evil.

Eating Matzah: *Motzi Matzah*

"To eat bread without hope is still slowly to starve to death."—PEARL S. BUCK

BUDDHIST MEAL GATHA (HYMN)

We receive this food
in gratitude to all beings

Who have helped to bring it to our table,

And vow to respond in turn to
those in need

With wisdom and compassion.

"All sorrows are less with bread."—MIGUEL DE CERVANTES

Bread is a staple food for many of us, but during Passover we eat matzah instead. This matzah reminds us how the Israelites left Egypt in such a hurry that they didn't have time to let their dough rise. Instead, the dough baked into matzah in the hot sun. Since matzah is a simple food, just flour and water, it also reminds us to appreciate the simple things in our lives.

Recite these two blessings. The first one is for bread, which represents all the food that we eat. The second blessing is recited for matzah.

Praised are You, Holy One, Sovereign of the universe, who brings forth bread from the earth.

Baruch Atah, Adonai Eloheinu, Melech ha'olam, hamotzi lechem min ha'aretz.

בָּרוּךְ אַתָּה יְיָ אֱלֹהֵינוּ מֶלֶךְ הָעוֹלָם, הַמּוֹצִיא לֶחֶם מִן הָאָרֶץ.

Praised are You, Holy One, Sovereign of the universe, who makes us holy with commandments and instructs us to eat matzah.

Baruch Atah, Adonai Eloheinu, Melech ha'olam, asher kid'shanu b'mitzvotav v'tzivanu al achilat matzah.

בָּרוּךְ אַתָּה יְיָ אֱלֹהֵינוּ מֶלֶךְ הָעוֹלָם, אֲשֶׁר קִדְּשָׁנוּ בְּמִצְוֹתָיו וְצִוָּנוּ עַל אֲכִילַת מַצָּה.

Now take your first taste of matzah. Eat it slowly. Take note of how it tastes.

Don't worry about the crumbs!

A CHRISTIAN GRACE BEFORE MEALS

Blessed be the Earth for providing us this food

Blessed be the Sun for helping it to grow

Blessed be the Wind and Birds for carrying its seed

Blessed be the Rain for the water's loving flow.

Blessed be the hands that helped prepare this meal,

May those hands and our hands, bodies too, be well and quick to heal.

Blessed be our friends, our families, and all of our loved ones.

Blessed be our mother earth, our father sky and sun.

The Bitterness of Slavery: *Maror*

"A person who takes a walk of one hundred feet and a person who walks two thousand miles have one major thing in common. They both need to take a first step before they take a second step."
—RABBI ZELIG PLISKIN

We eat bitter herbs, often horseradish or romaine lettuce, to remember the bitterness of slavery. And it's all too easy to feel our own bitterness at times. As we complete this ritual of *maror*, we embrace all that we have received—the good with the bad. The choice is ours: we can be bitter with our lot, or we can focus with gratitude on what is good in our lives.

Take a piece of horseradish or other bitter herb. Some people dip it in *charoset* **to sweeten the taste. Then read the words below:**

Praised are You, Holy One, Sovereign of the universe, who makes us holy with commandments and instructs us to eat bitter herbs.

Baruch Atah, Adonai Eloheinu, Melech ha'olam, asher kid'shanu b'mitzvotav v'tzivanu al achilat maror.

בָּרוּךְ אַתָּה יְיָ אֱלֹהֵינוּ מֶלֶךְ הָעוֹלָם, אֲשֶׁר קִדְּשָׁנוּ בְּמִצְוֹתָיו וְצִוָּנוּ עַל אֲכִילַת מָרוֹר.

After you have said the words of blessing, notice the taste of the bitter herb. Let the flavors and the bitterness roll over your tongue.

THE SERENITY PRAYER (WITH HEBREW TRANSLATION)

The Serenity Prayer has become an important part of daily reflections for many people. Read each word slowly, focusing on the meaning or the sound of it. You might ask participants to read the Hebrew translation or the English, or both, responsively.

God, grant me the serenity

Eli tein li et hashalvah

to accept the things I cannot change,

l'kabeil et had'varim she'ein bicholti l'shanotam

courage to change the things I can,

ometz l'shanot et had'varim asher bicholti

and wisdom to know the difference.

v'et hat'vunah l'havchin bein hash'nayim.

—Reinhold Niebuhr

Sandwiching the Bitter: *Koreich*

"The antonym to despair is hope; the path to get there is through bitterness."—RABBI MARK BOROVITZ

Throughout history, the Jewish people have lived in many lands, from ancient Babylonia (now Iraq) to the far reaches of Europe, Asia, and Africa. Sometimes Jews traveled in search of opportunity, freedom, and safety. Sometimes they were forced to leave. In every land in which they lived, Jews interacted with the local culture, including its cuisine, absorbed it, and tried to make it their own. In so doing they transformed the bitter into sweet.

In ancient times, the great teacher Rabbi Hillel combined *maror* with *charoset*, sandwiching the bitter with the sweet. We continue this custom now by eating a Hillel sandwich.

Distribute pieces of the bottom matzah. Invite participants to place a piece of *maror* and some *charoset* between two pieces of matzah. Enjoy!

DIFFERENT KINDS OF CHAROSET

Different families and communities may have their own recipes for *charoset*, often influenced by local ingredients. Turn to page 54 for a Roasted Peanut *Charoset* recipe from the Abayudaya community in Uganda. You'll also find *charoset* from Italy, with its unusual and tasty notes of cocoa and vanilla. What is your favorite kind of *charoset*? Take a vote around the table to find out the most popular kind.

Holiday Meal: *Shulchan Oreich*

"So long as you have food in your mouth,
you have solved all questions for the time being."
—FRANZ KAFKA

Many families begin their Passover meal with an egg. There are many explanations for this tradition. The egg is the same symbol of life that appears in other Jewish rituals and traditions, as well as in other faith traditions. At Passover, the egg is also a connection to spring. Some people dip their egg in salt water—a symbol of tears—connecting it to the rituals of dipping earlier in the seder.

It's time to enjoy a festive meal!

A SHAKER HYMN

Lord, prepare me to be a sanctuary

Pure and holy, tried and true

With thanksgiving, I'll be a living

Sanctuary for You.

A MUSLIM PRAYER BEFORE EATING

Muslims begin a meal with the Arabic words, *Bismallah Alrahman Alraheem*, which means "In the name of God, the most gracious, the most merciful [do we eat]."

The Afikoman: *Tzafun*

"There is no hiding 'in the dark,' either from God or from ourselves."—RABBI AMY R. SCHEINERMAN

The *afikoman* is the name given to the middle matzah that we broke and hid earlier in the seder. Invite everyone, especially the children, to find the *afikoman*. Be prepared to offer a reward for its return. Then break off pieces to share with everyone at the table. This is the last taste of the seder meal and it provides us with a lasting taste of the seder experience.

Expressing Gratitude: *Bareich*

"Human beings must act in order to bring about a more perfect world."—RABBI AMMIEL HIRSCH

G ratitude goes beyond an appreciation for this evening that we have spent together. It is a lens through which we can view our daily lives—even the most routine activities. When we express our thanks for the things with which we have been blessed, it enhances our awareness of those blessings. When we express our appreciation for the meal we have eaten and for the friendship and family we have enjoyed, this brings us closer to our own selves and to one another.

Fill your glass—for the third time—with grape juice or wine. Then together repeat the following words slowly, in Aramaic. This text from the Talmud is offered here in place of the Birkat Hamazon, the traditional blessing after meals.

Praised is the Merciful One, Ruler of the world, Creator of this bread.

B'rich rachamana malka di alma marei d'hai pita.

The Third Cup

"As Jews we come together in our most vulnerable moments . . . . As black folks we have come to the street, to the courthouse, to the town square to demand justice . . . . When we say Black Lives Matter we are calling for the recognition of God in us all. We are calling for our skin to be recognized as the skin of family, our tears to be recognized as the tears of mothers, of fathers, of lovers, the tears of God . . . . We are a people centered in loss and justice. We are a people who know that there is a better world and that it is our responsibility, our duty to love and support one another. The stranger, the beggar, and the familial . . . ."

—Graie Barasch–Hagans

The third cup of wine or grape juice that we drink corresponds to God's third promise to free the Israelites from slavery.

Fill your glass, then raise it while reciting the third promise:

"I will redeem you with an outstretched arm." (Exodus 6:6)

Get comfortable, then say the blessing:

Praised are You, Holy One, Sovereign of the universe, who creates the fruit of the vine.

Baruch Atah, Adonai Eloheinu, Melech ha'olam, borei p'ri hagafen.

בָּרוּךְ אַתָּה יְיָ אֱלֹהֵינוּ מֶלֶךְ הָעוֹלָם, בּוֹרֵא פְּרִי הַגָּפֶן.

Now you may drink the wine or grape juice.

Elijah the Prophet

Ask a participant to open the door of the house. Then point to Elijah's Cup.

This is Elijah's Cup. We set aside this cup and open the door to our home to welcome Elijah the Prophet, who, according to Jewish tradition, will announce the coming of the Messiah. The messianic time is said to be a more perfect world, free from judgment and persecution and war. We can work toward that vision now by creating spaces where anybody who wants to participate in the Jewish community is celebrated and welcomed. This seder is one of those spaces.

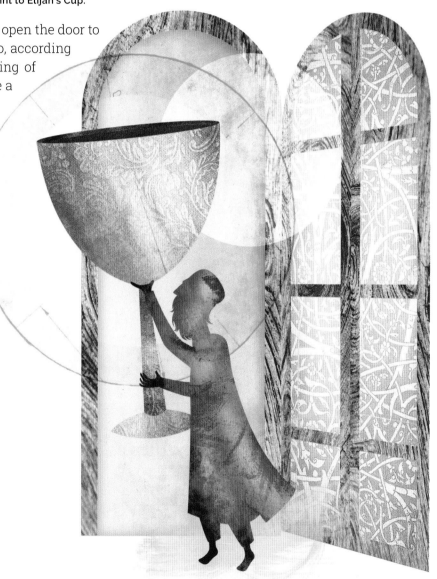

We fill Elijah's Cup together to acknowledge that Elijah will not come until we work together to bring about more justice in the world.

Ask each participant to pour a little wine or grape juice from his or her own cup into Elijah's Cup. Then close the door.

Watch your fingers!

"Hope is like peace. It is not a gift from God. It is a gift only we can give one another."
—Elie Wiesel

Giving Praise: *Hallel*

"Hang on to the name(s) for God that are meaningful for you, that help you pray with God, and that help you connect with your faith community.... All these names of God point to one God."—SISTER JULIE VIEIRA

There are numerous occasions for wonder and awe in the world, but we aren't always conscious of them as we go about our daily routines. Reciting the Hallel psalms can help us to recognize these occasions. Alternatively, you may form your own expression of thanksgiving.

God is with me, so I am not afraid; what can humans do to me? . . . .

A joyful shout of triumph rings in the tents of the righteous . . . .

Open the gates of righteousness for me so that I may enter through them . . . .

The stone that the builders rejected has become the foundation stone. (from Psalm 118)

The Fourth Cup

The fourth cup of wine or grape juice that we drink tonight corresponds to God's fourth promise to free the Israelites from their slavery.

Fill your glass, then raise it while reciting the fourth promise:

"I will take you to be My people, and I will be your God."
(Exodus 6:7)

Stretch out. Get comfortable. Say the blessing:

Praised are You, Holy One, Sovereign of the universe, who creates the fruit of the vine.

Baruch Atah, Adonai Eloheinu, Melech ha'olam, borei p'ri hagafen.

בָּרוּךְ אַתָּה יְיָ אֱלֹהֵינוּ מֶלֶךְ הָעוֹלָם, בּוֹרֵא פְּרִי הַגָּפֶן.

Now drink the wine or grape juice.

Our seder is nearly complete. We have turned an evening meal into a celebration of memory and community, and our challenge now is to take this moment and carry it with us after we leave, so that we can continue to see the sacred in the routine of daily life.

" To sing the songs of *Hallel* in the desert is, perhaps, to have half a smile. It is to look around the wilderness, the imperfect world, our imperfect lives—and still say: *Halleluyah.*"

—Rabbi Sari Laufer

Seeking Acceptance: *Nirtzah*

"Even after the Lord had delivered the Israelites from Egypt, they had to travel through the desert.... We must be ready.... Let us be united, let us be filled with hope, let us be those who respect one another."—ARCHBISHOP DESMOND TUTU

The presence of all us gathered around this table brings us closer to the final promise of the seder—redemption. The world will be redeemed through acts of goodness, beginning with embracing all those who join us tonight. Through our coming together, may we all be redeemed.

We say together the following words, which represent an expression of solidarity with the Jewish people and a longing for spiritual redemption:

Next year in Jerusalem!

L'shanah haba'ah biY'rushalayim!

לְשָׁנָה הַבָּאָה בִּירוּשָׁלָיִם.

ORAH HI: SHE IS LIGHT

*A Feminist Alternative
to Adir Hu*

She is light, she is light.

(Refrain:)
**May She build her house speedily
and in our days.**

**God, build Your house soon—close to
us in time and space.**

(Repeat refrain after each line below.)

She is wisdom, She is joy, She is tears...

She is splendor, She is a rose,
She is a flowing stream...

She is renewal, She is the center,
She is oneness...

She is the full moon, She is birth,
She is the fountain-source...

She is comfort, She is forgiveness,
She is strength...

She is redemption,
She is righteousness, She is holiness...

She is a beloved companion,
She is always changing,
She is complete and perfect...

Orah hi, orah hi,
(Refrain:)
***Tivnei veitah b'karov,
bimherah, bimherah,
b'yameinu b'karov,***

***elah b'ni, elah b'ni,
b'ni veiteich b'karov.***

(Repeat refrain after each line below.)

Binah hi, gilah hi, dimah hi...

Hadar hi, vered hi, zerem hi...

Chiddush hi, tibur hi, yichud hi...

Keseh hi, leidah hi, ma'yan hi...

Nechamah hi, selichah hi, otzmah hi...

Pidyon hi, tzedek hi, kodesh hi...

Ra'ya hi, shonah hi, tamah hi...

—Rabbi Jill Hammer

Seder Songs

Adir Hu: God Is Mighty

The words used to praise God in this song form an alphabetical acrostic in Hebrew, starting with all the letters of the Hebrew alphabet.

God is Mighty, God is Mighty.

(Refrain:)
May God build the Temple soon,

Speedily in our time, soon.

**Build it, Eternal One! Build it,
Eternal One!**

(Repeat refrain after each
line below.)

God is supreme, great, outstanding...

God is glorious, faithful, worthy...

God is kind, pure, unique...

God is mighty, wise, majestic...

God is awesome, strong, powerful...

God is redeeming, righteous, holy...

God is compassionate, almighty,
resolute...

Adir hu, adir hu

(Refrain:)
Yivneh veito b'karov

***bimherah, bimherah
b'yameinu b'karov***

***El b'neih, El b'neih
b'neih veit'cha b'karov.***

(Repeat refrain after each
line below.)

Bachur hu, gadol hu, dagul hu...

Hadur hu, vatik hu, zakai hu...

Chasid hu, tahor hu, yachid hu...

Kabir hu, lamud hu, melech hu...

Nora hu, sagiv hu, izuz hu...

Podeh hu, tzadik hu, kadosh hu...

Rachum hu, Shadai hu, takif hu...

Echad Mi Yodei'a: Who Knows One?

Who knows one? *I know one.*
One is our God in heaven and on earth.

Who knows two? *I know two.*
Two are the tablets of the Covenant.
One is our God in heaven and
on earth.

Who knows three? *I know three.*
Three are the patriarchs.
Two are the tablets of the Covenant.
One is our God in heaven and
on earth.

(continue as above)

Four are the matriarchs.

Five are the books of the Torah.

Six are the sections of the Mishnah.

Seven are the days of the week.

Eight are the days to circumcision.

Nine are the months to childbirth.

Ten are the Commandments.

Eleven are the stars in Joseph's dream.

Twelve are the tribes of Israel.

Thirteen are the attributes of God.

Echad mi yodei'a? *Echad
ani yodei'a: Echad Eloheinu
shebashamayim uva'aretz.*

Sh'nayim mi yodei'a? *Sh'nayim ani
yodei'a: Sh'nei luchot habrit, echad
Eloheinu shebashamayim uva'aretz.*

Sh'loshah mi yodei'a? *Sh'loshah
ani yodei'a: Sh'loshah avot, sh'nei
luchot habrit, echad Eloheinu
shebashamayim uva'aretz.*

Arba mi yodei'a? *Arba ani yodei'a:
Arba imahot, sh'loshah avot, sh'nei
luchot habrit, echad Eloheinu
shebashamayim uva'aretz.*

Chamishah mi yodei'a? *Chamishah
ani yodei'a: Chamishah chumshei
Torah, arba imahot, sh'loshah avot,
sh'nei luchot habrit, echad Eloheinu
shebashamayim uva'aretz.*

Shishah mi yodei'a? *Shishah ani
yodei'a: Shishah sidrei Mishnah,
chamishah chumshei Torah, arba
imahot, sh'loshah avot, sh'nei
luchot habrit, echad Eloheinu
shebashamayim uva'aretz.*

Shiv'ah mi yodei'a? *Shiv'ah ani
yodei'a: Shiv'ah y'mei Shabta,
shishah sidrei Mishnah, chamishah
chumshei Torah, arba imahot,
sh'loshah avot, sh'nei luchot habrit,
echad Eloheinu shebashamayim
uva'aretz.*

Sh'monah mi yodei'a? *Sh'monah
ani yodei'a: Sh'monah y'mei milah,
shiv'ah y'mei Shabta, shishah sidrei
Mishnah, chamishah chumshei
Torah, arba imahot, sh'loshah avot,
sh'nei luchot habrit, echad Eloheinu
shebashamayim uva'aretz.*

Tish'ah mi yodei'a? *Tish'ah ani
yodei'a: Tish'ah yarchei leidah,
sh'monah y'mei milah, shiv'ah
y'mei Shabta, shishah sidrei
Mishnah, chamishah chumshei
Torah, arba imahot, sh'loshah avot,
sh'nei luchot habrit, echad Eloheinu
shebashamayim uva'aretz.*

Asarah mi yodei'a? *Asarah ani
yodei'a: Asarah dibraya, tish'ah
yarchei leidah, sh'monah y'mei
milah, shiv'ah y'mei Shabta,
shishah sidrei Mishnah, chamishah
chumshei Torah, arba imahot,
sh'loshah avot, sh'nei luchot habrit,
echad Eloheinu shebashamayim
uva'aretz.*

Achad asar mi yodei'a? *Achad asar
ani yodei'a: Achad asar kochvaya,
asarah dibraya, tish'ah yarchei
leidah, sh'monah y'mei milah,
shiv'ah y'mei Shabta, shishah sidrei
Mishnah, chamishah chumshei
Torah, arba imahot, sh'loshah avot,
sh'nei luchot habrit, echad Eloheinu
shebashamayim uva'aretz.*

Sh'neim asar mi yodei'a? *Sh'neim
asar ani yodei'a: Sh'neim asar
shivtaya, achad asar kochvaya,
asarah dibraya, tish'ah yarchei
leidah, sh'monah y'mei milah,
shiv'ah y'mei Shabta, shishah sidrei
Mishnah, chamishah chumshei
Torah, arba imahot, sh'loshah avot,
sh'nei luchot habrit, echad Eloheinu
shebashamayim uva'aretz.*

Sh'loshah asar mi yodei'a?
*Sh'loshah asar ani yodei'a:
Sh'loshah asar midaya, sh'neim
asar shivtaya, achad asar kochvaya,
asarah dibraya, tish'ah yarchei
leidah, sh'monah y'mei milah,
shiv'ah y'mei Shabta, shishah sidrei
Mishnah, chamishah chumshei
Torah, arba imahot, sh'loshah avot,
sh'nei luchot habrit, echad Eloheinu
shebashamayim uva'aretz.*

Chad Gadya: One Little Goat

One little goat, one little goat, my father bought for two *zuzim, chad gadya, chad gadya.*

Then came the cat that ate the goat my father bought for two *zuzim, chad gadya, chad gadya.*

Then came the dog that bit the cat that ate the goat my father bought for two *zuzim, chad gadya, chad gadya.*

(continue as above)

Then came the stick that beat the dog . . .

Then came the fire that burned the stick . . .

Then came the water that quenched the fire . . .

Then came the ox that drank the water . . .

Then came the butcher that killed the ox . . .

Then came the angel of death that slew the butcher . . .

(final verse)
Then came the Holy One that destroyed the angel of death that slew the butcher that killed the ox that drank the water that quenched the fire that burned the stick that beat the dog that bit the cat that ate the goat my father bought for two *zuzim, chad gadya, chad gadya.*

Chad gadya, chad gadya, dizvan aba bitrei zuzei, chad gadya, chad gadya.

V'ata shun'ra, v'ach'lah l'gadya, dizvan aba bitrei zuzei, chad gadya, chad gadya.

V'ata chalba, v'nashach l'shun'ra, d'ach'lah l'gadya, dizvan aba bitrei zuzei, chad gadya, chad gadya.

V'ata chut'ra, v'hikah l'chalba, d'nashach l'shun'ra, d'ach'lah l'gadya, dizvan aba bitrei zuzei, chad gadya, chad gadya.

V'ata nura, v'saraf l'chut'ra, d'hikah l'chalba, d'nashach l'shun'ra, d'ach'lah l'gadya, dizvan aba bitrei zuzei, chad gadya, chad gadya.

V'ata maya, v'chavah l'nura, d'saraf l'chut'ra, d'hikah l'chalba, d'nashach l'shun'ra, d'ach'lah l'gadya, dizvan aba bitrei zuzei, chad gadya, chad gadya.

V'ata tora, v'shata l'maya, d'chavah l'nura, d'saraf l'chut'ra, d'hikah l'chalba, d'nashach l'shun'ra, d'ach'lah l'gadya, dizvan aba bitrei zuzei, chad gadya, chad gadya.

V'ata hashocheit, v'shachat l'tora, d'shata l'maya, d'chavah l'nura, d'saraf l'chut'ra, d'hikah l'chalba, d'nashach l'shun'ra, d'ach'lah l'gadya, dizvan aba bitrei zuzei, chad gadya, chad gadya.

V'ata malach hamavet, v'shachat l'shocheit, d'shachat l'tora, d'shata l'maya, d'chavah l'nura, d'saraf l'chut'ra, d'hikah l'chalba, d'nashach l'shun'ra, d'ach'lah l'gadya, dizvan aba bitrei zuzei, chad gadya, chad gadya.

V'ata haKadosh Baruch Hu, v'shachat l'malach hamavet, d'shachat l'shocheit, d'shachat l'tora, d'shata l'maya, d'chavah l'nura, d'saraf l'chut'ra, d'hikah l'chalba, d'nashach l'shun'ra, d'ach'lah l'gadya, dizvan aba bitrei zuzei, chad gadya, chad gadya.

Let My People Go

(Refrain:)
Go down Moses, way down to Egypt land
Tell old Pharaoh, "Let my people go!"

When Israel was in Egypt Land
Let my people go!
They worked so hard they could not stand
Let my people go!

(Refrain)

Then God told Moses what to do
Let my people go!
To lead the children of Israel through
Let my people go!

(Refrain)

Israelites were scared, didn't know what to do
Let my people go!
But slavery hurt and this they knew
Let me people go!

(Refrain)

They traveled through the desert for forty years
Let my people go!
With God on their side they had nothing to fear
Let my people go!

(Refrain)

The Israelites learned what it meant to be free
Let my people go!
The world's big enough for you and me
Let my people go!

—Traditional Spiritual, Additional Lyrics
by Shira Kline

Seder Recipes

Ingredients

4 cups roasted peanuts

3 apples, finely chopped

2 bananas, chopped into small pieces

1/2 cup sweet wine (or grape juice)

1/2 cup honey

Roasted Peanut *Charoset*

This recipe comes from the Abayudaya community in Uganda, where peanuts are plentiful. If you don't eat peanuts during Passover or are allergic to them, you may replace the peanuts with cashews.

Directions

Grind the peanuts in a blender and place them in a medium-sized bowl. Or use a mortar and pestle as local Ugandans do. Mix with the chopped apples and bananas. Add the wine and stir. Then mix in the honey. You can thicken the mixture by adding more honey.

—Tziporah Sizomu

Ingredients

1/2 pound pitted dates

1/2 pound walnuts

3 large apples, peeled and cored

1 large whole seedless orange, washed and cut into chunks

3 large ripe bananas

1/3 cup sweet wine

1/2 teaspoon cinnamon

1/8 teaspoon ground cloves

1 tablespoon lemon juice

Matzah meal as needed

1/4 cup unsweetened cocoa

1/4 cup vanilla-flavored sugar

Italian *Charoset*

This recipe really tells a story. The Ottoman influence is seen with the dates, walnuts, and spices. The apples represent the immigrants from the north of Italy. The citrus fruits signal the presence of Jews in the citrus industry in Italy, and the cocoa and vanilla have come from the Jewish traders who lived in South and Central America.

Directions

1. Place the dates, apples, walnuts, and orange chunks in a processor and process until very fine. Spoon into a medium bowl.

2. Peel and mash the bananas, and add to the other mixture in bowl.

3. Add the wine, spices, and lemon juice and mix well. If the mixture is too moist or soft, then add a few tablespoons of matzah meal to the fruit mixture. Wait 10 minutes before proceeding so that the matzah meal can hydrate and absorb any excess moisture.

4. Mix together the cocoa and vanilla-flavored sugar.

5. Make little balls out of the paste. Roll them in the cocoa-sugar mixture just before serving.

Yield: 3–4 dozen balls

—Tina Wasserman, *Entrée to Judaism*

Make Your Own Matzah

Matzah is readily available in most supermarkets, but if you
like to bake, and you have the time, try making your own matzah.
It can be a fun activity in the days before Passover.

Ingredients

1/2 cup cold water

1 1/2 cups flour

additional flour, as needed

Directions

1. Set 4 unglazed tiles, or a pizza stone or heavy baking sheet,
   on the top rack of the oven. Preheat the oven to 500 degrees,
   or its highest temperature.

2. Set a timer for 18 minutes. To make kosher-for-Passover matzah,
   no more than 18 minutes may pass from when the water touches
   the flour until the matzah is done.

3. Combine flour and water and knead quickly until the dough is
   smooth and no longer sticky.

4. Divide the dough into four equal balls, and roll each one out with a
   rolling pin, dusting with flour if needed. Roll out until the dough is no
   more than 1/8" thick. (This is a great activity to do in a small group,
   with each person rolling out one of the balls of dough, to save time.)

5. Prick holes all over the dough with a fork or a tracing wheel.
   Turn the dough over and prick the other side. This will help it bake
   more quickly and thoroughly.

5. Bake on the tiles for 2–4 minutes, until brown and crisp.
   Cool on a wire rack.

Sources. THE AUTHOR GRATEFULLY ACKNOWLEDGES THE FOLLOWING SOURCES.

"Bismillah al rahman al rahim." Wahiduddin's Web. January 3, 2008. https://wahiduddin.net/words/bismillah.htm.

"Confucius>Quotes>Quotable Quote." Goodreads. https://www.goodreads.com/quotes/79127-if-your-plan-is-for-one-year-plant-rice-if (accessed September 20, 2017).

Barasch-Hagans, Graie. Black Lives Matter Haggadah, Unabridged Version. New York City, NY: Jews For Racial & Economic Justice, 2015. Reprinted with permission.

Barenblat, Rabbi Rachel. The Velveteen Rabbi's Haggadah for Pesach. February 3, 2015. https://velveteenrabbi.com/2015/02/03/velveteen-rabbis-haggadah-for-pesach/. Reprinted with permission.

Borovitz, Rabbi Mark. "Rabbi Mark Borovitz." Beit T'Shuvah. September 4, 2012. https://beittshuvah.wordpress.com/author/holythief/.

Buck, Pearl S. To My Daughters, With Love. New York, NY: J. Day, 1967.

Copeland, Rabbi Mychal. "Torah | Valuing our broken pieces allows us to become whole." J. The Jewish News of Northern California. April 18, 2014. https://www.jweekly.com/2014/04/18/torah-valuing-our-broken-pieces-allows-us-to-become-whole/.

Creditor, Rabbi Menachem. "How Much Longer, Wendy's?" PDF. T'ruah: The Rabbinic Call for Human Rights. http://www.truah.org/wp-content/uploads/2017/03/SHabbat_kavanah_CIW_solidarity_fast.pdf.

De Cervantes Saavedra, Miguel. Don Quixote. New York, NY: Penguin Classics, 2003.

Feld, Merle. Finding Words. New York: URJ Press, 2011. Used with permission of the author.

Franken, Kris. "Bless This Food: The Healthy Ritual of Giving Thanks." http://www.krisfranken.com/2017/02/bless-this-food-give-thanks/ (accessed September 18, 2017).

Greenberg, Sara. "The Real Meaning of Dayenu." Jewish Exponent. January 25, 2017. http://jewishexponent.com/2013/04/01/the-real-meaning-of-dayenu/. Reprinted with permission.

Gropper, Rabbi Daniel. "Seder at Bnei Brak." Haggadot.com. https://www.haggadot.com/clip/seder-bnei-brak (accessed August 09, 2017). Reprinted with permission.

Hammer, Rabbi Jill. "Orah Hi: A New Passover Hymn." Tel Shemesh: Celebrating and Creating Earth-Based Traditions in Judaism. 2008. http://telshemesh.org/nisan/orah_hi_a_new_passover_hymn.html. Reprinted with permission.

Hirsch, Ammiel, and Yosef Reinman. One People, Two Worlds: A Reform Rabbi and an Orthodox Rabbi Explore the Issues That Divide Them. New York, NY: Knopf Doubleday Publishing Group, 2002.

Hobbins, John. "The Serenity Prayer in Hebrew Patiently Explained." Ancient Hebrew Poetry. June 26, 2008. http://ancienthebrewpoetry.typepad.com/ancient_hebrew_poetry/2008/06/the-serenity-prayer-in-hebrew-patiently-explained.html.

Hoover, Heidi. "Ruth's Cup: A New Passover Ritual Honoring Jewish Diversity." My Jewish Learning. March 30, 2017. http://www.myjewishlearning.com/jewish-and/ruths-cup-a-new-passover-ritual-honoring-jewish-diversity/.

Kafka, Franz. The Trial, America, In the Penal Settlement, Metamorphosis, The Castle, The Great Wall of China, Investigations of a Dog, Letter to His Father, The Diaries 1910-23. London: Secker & Warburg, 1976.

Kennedy, John F. "John F. Kennedy: Radio and Television Report to the American People on Civil Rights," June 11, 1963. John F. Kennedy Presidential Library and Museum. https://www.jfklibrary.org/Research/Research-Aids/JFK-Speeches/Civil-Rights-Radio-and-Television-Report_19630611.aspx.

King, Martin Luther, and James Melvin. A Testament f Hope: The Essential Writings and Speeches of Martin Luther King, Jr. San Francisco: HarperSanFrancisco, 1991.

Kline, Shira. ShirLaLa Pesach! Lyrics and Guitar Chords. DOC. www.ShirLaLa.com. Reprinted with permission.

Laufer, Rabbi Sari. "Nothing on Our Tongues but Halleluyah: A Shabbat Hagadol/Passover Drash." TorahBlahnik. April 10, 2017. http://torahblahnik.blogspot.com/2017/.

Loori, John Daido. Celebrating Everyday Life: Zen Home Liturgy. Mt. Tremper, NY: Dharma Communications, 1999.

Mandela, Nelson. Long Walk to Freedom: the Autobiography of Nelson Mandela. Paw Prints, 2014.

Morinis, Alan. "What Makes Us Happy? A Symposium." Moment. October 8, 2014. http://www.momentmag.com/makes-us-happy-symposium/. Reprinted with permission of Dr. Alan Morinis, Dean, The Mussar Institute www.mussarinstitute.org.

Niebuhr, Reinhold. "The Serenity Prayer." Origin of the prayer is unknown, although it is often attributed to Reinhold Niebuhr, who used it in a sermon in 1934. For more information see "The Origin of Our Serenity Prayer." http://www.aahistory.com/prayer.html.

Pakuda, Bachya ibn. Hobot HaLebabot. Eleventh century.

Pliskin, Rabbi Zelig. Aish.com. January 18, 2015. http://www.aish.com/sp/pg/7-Inspiring-Jewish-Quotes.html.

Ramer, Andrew and Mark Horn. The Stonewall Shabbat Seder. New York City: Congregation B'nai Jeshurun, 1997. Used with permission.

Raphael, Rabbi Geela Rayzel. "Five Interfaith Passover Readings You Can Add to Your Hagaddah." InterfaithFamily. March 28, 2006. http://www.interfaithfamily.com/holidays/passover_and_easter/Five_Interfaith_Passover_Readings_You_Can_Add_to_Your_Hagaddah.shtml.

Scheinerman, Rabbi Amy R. "Elul Week 1 - Responsibility." http://scheinerman.net/judaism/hhd/teshuvah/psalm27-1.html (accessed September 19, 2017).

Schnur, Rabbi Susan. A Miriam Seder: Remembering and Celebrating the Heroines of Passover. Boston, MA: Central Reform Temple of Boston, 2013. Reprinted with permission from Lilith magazine--independent, Jewish & frankly feminist. More at Lilith.org.

Shaker Hymn is based on a Hebrew verse from the Book of Exodus. For more information see Barenblat, Rabbi Rachel. "Song of the Month: Tishri 5772/ October 2011" CBI: From the Rabbi. https://congregationbethisrael.wordpress.com/2011/10/10/song-of-the-month-tishri-5772-october-2011/.

Sizomu, Tziporah. "Tziporah's Charoset Recipe ." Global Jews. March 26, 2010. http://bechollashon.org/heart/index.php/articles/3868. Reprinted with permission.

Strassfeld, Michael. A Book of Life: Embracing Judaism as a Spiritual Practice. Woodstock, VT: Jewish Lights Pub., 2012. Reprinted with permission of the author.

Thales of Miletus. "'Water is the beginning of all things.' – Thales of Miletus, 600 B.C." The Roger Tory Peterson Institute of Natural History. July 28, 2015. http://rtpi.org/water-is-the-beginning-of-all-things-thales-of-miletus-600-b-c/.

Tutu, Archbishop Desmond, quote from Rosin, Joseph H. Haggadah: Passover Seder Freedom Celebration. Largo, FL: Joseph H. Rosin, 2009.

Viera, Sister Julie. "Why does God have so many names?" A Nun's Life Ministry. July 7, 2014. https://anunslife.org/blog/nun-talk/why-does-god-have-so-many-names.

Wasserman, Tina. Entrée to Judaism: A Culinary Exploration of the Jewish Diaspora. New York: URJ Press, 2010. Reprinted with permission.

Wiesel, Elie. "Elie Wiesel Quotes." BrainyQuote. http://www.mccc.edu/~degiorge/ElieWiesel.htm (accessed September 18, 2017).

Williamson, Marianne. "Christmas for Mystics." https://marianne.com/christmas-for-mystics/ (accessed August 09, 2017).

Zukav, Gary. "Gary Zukav on Spiritual Spring Cleaning." Huffington Post.com. May 18, 2012. http://www.huffingtonpost.com/gary-zukav/gary-zukav-on-spiritual-s_b_1528194.html.